KIDS PLAYING SOCCER
IN BHUTAN

LITTLE KIDS
FIRST
BiG
BOOK OF
SPORTS

James Buckley, Jr.

NATIONAL
GEOGRAPHIC
KiDS

WASHINGTON, D.C.

Contents

Introduction 6

How to Use This Book 7

What Is a Sport? 8

CHAPTER ONE

The Big Five 10

Basketball 12

Football 18

Baseball
and Softball 24

Soccer 30

Ice Hockey 36

CHAPTER TWO

Team Sports 42

Field Hockey 44

Lacrosse 46

Cheerleading 48

Rugby 50

Cricket 52

Ultimate 54

Volleyball 56

Playground Sports 58

CHAPTER THREE

Individual Sports 60

Archery 62

Bowling 64

Wrestling 66

Cycling 68

Fencing 70

Golf 72

Tennis 74

More Racket Sports 76

Rock Climbing 78

Gymnastics 80

Karate 82

Surfing 84

Swimming and Diving 86

More Water Sports 88

Skateboarding 90

Track and Field 92

Motorsports 96

CHAPTER FOUR

Snow and Ice	**98**
Curling	100
Figure Skating	102
Speed Skating	104
Skiing	106
Snowboarding	108
Sledding	110

CHAPTER FIVE

The Olympics	**112**
Summer Olympics	114
Winter Olympics	116
Paralympics	118
Special Olympics	120

Map: Even More Sports	**122**
Parent Tips	**124**
Glossary and Additional Resources	**125**
Index	**126**
Photo Credits	**127**
Acknowledgments	**128**

Introduction

Get ready to play! In this book, we'll take a look at many different sports around the world and how they are played. Sports bring people together to play, watch, and cheer for their favorite teams and athletes. Whether the sport needs a ball or a stick, a pool or a field, a racket or a ski pole, young readers can explore each sport's history and the rules and skills that make that sport unique!

Chapter One focuses on the "Big Five" most popular worldwide sports. Basketball and soccer are played in just about every country on Earth. Football is played mostly in the United States and Canada. Ice hockey, baseball, and softball started in North America but are now played around the world.

Chapter Two takes a look at many other team sports, including cricket, rugby, field hockey, lacrosse, volleyball, and ultimate frisbee (known as ultimate). It also introduces some playground games from around the world.

Chapter Three introduces popular individual sports. These activities—from archery to bowling to skateboarding to diving—challenge each athlete to do their best all by themselves.

Chapter Four explores a variety of sports played on snow and ice, from curling to skating to sledding.

Chapter Five covers the Olympic Games, the Paralympics, and the Special Olympics. It wraps up with a variety of sports that are played around the planet.

How to Use This Book

Colorful photographs illustrate each spread and support the text.

Fact boxes give young readers bits of sports history, information about gear and rules, sports lingo, and fun trivia.

Archery

INDIVIDUAL SPORTS

A "Robin Hood" is when an archer splits an arrow down its center by firing another arrow into it.

FACTS

The part at the back of the arrow is called the fletching. It helps steer the arrow as it flies through the air.

The straight part of the arrow is called the shaft.

The bag that archers use to hold their arrows is called a quiver.

A peeker is an archer who aims the bow and then lowers it to look at the target again.

Hold out a thumbtack as far as you can. That tack is how small the bull's-eye looks to an Olympic archer!

This is one of the oldest sports in this book! Humans created the bow and arrow more than 60,000 years ago to hunt for food. Today, the sport of archery uses the same technique. Archers put an arrow in the bow, pull back the bowstring, aim for the target, and release the arrow.

Archers aim their arrow at a target that has 10 rings. Each ring is worth a different number of points. The ring in the center, called the bull's-eye, is worth 10 points.

Can you pretend to aim an arrow at a target? Try it!

62

63

Interactive questions in each section encourage conversation related to the topic.

The back of the book offers **parent tips** that include fun sports-related activities, along with a helpful **glossary.**

Pop-up facts throughout provide added information about the featured sports.

What Is a Sport?

Big or small, short or tall, people love to play. We play outside and we play inside. We play by ourselves and we play together. Playing is a natural part of being a person!

Over the years, some of the ways we play were organized into sports. The dictionary says that a sport is a physical activity with rules. A person or a group of people (a team) compete under those rules.

Cheering is a big part of sports! Even if you are not playing the sport, you can still thrill at watching athletes perform.

In this book, you'll read about all sorts of sports and how they are played. Then pick your favorites and try them out!

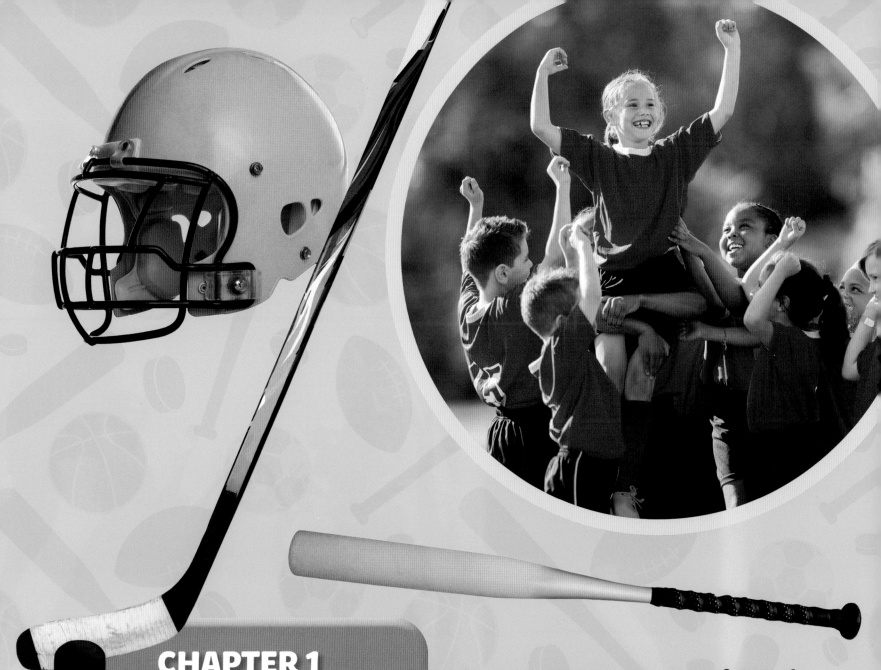

CHAPTER 1
The Big Five

In team sports, groups of people play against one another. The five team sports in this chapter are among the most popular in the world. Millions—even billions—of people play and watch them.

FACTS

Basketball is played indoors and outdoors.

When the ball goes through the hoop, it's called a basket.

Soccer balls were used as the first basketballs.

Basketball

In December 1891, a PE teacher in Massachusetts, U.S.A., needed an indoor game for his students to play during the winter. James Naismith wrote the rules for a new sport he called "basket ball." Many of his rules are still used today.

The playing area for basketball is called a court. There are two teams with five players each. Players score points by throwing, or "shooting," the ball through a tall hoop at each end of the court. The team that scores the most points wins.

James Naismith used empty peach baskets as the target for the ball.

How high can you jump?

A nickname for basketball is "hoops."

When a player is dribbling, another player can try to knock the ball away. This is called a steal.

A basketball game begins with a tip-off, or jump ball. The referee tosses the ball into the air. One player from each team jumps up and tries to tap the ball to a teammate.

Basketball players can only use their hands to move the ball around the court. They dribble the ball, bouncing it over and over with one hand. They also make passes to their teammates. The passes can go through the air or bounce first.

When a player shoots the ball and misses the hoop, any player can grab the ball. This is called getting a rebound. Or, *swish!* The ball goes through the hoop. Now the other team gets the ball. It's their turn to try to score.

In a layup, a player leaps near the basket and tosses the ball into the hoop.

15

The Basketball Court

RIM AND BACKBOARD

FREE THROW LINE

A player shoots the ball from the free throw line when the other team makes a foul.

Fouls include pushing or grabbing a player on the opposing team.

THREE POINT LINE

If a player makes a basket outside of the three point line, three points are scored.

SIDELINE

HALF-COURT LINE

The half-court line divides the court into two equal sections.

If one team throws the ball outside the sidelines, the other team throws it back into the court to restart play.

GET TO THE POINT

Field Goal (basket) . . . . 2 points

Field Goal Outside
  the Three Point Line . . . . 3 points

Free Throw . . . . 1 point

BASKET

CENTER CIRCLE

Players stand at center circle for the tip-off that starts the game.

LET'S PLAY!

You don't need an official court and a lot of people to play basketball. You just need a ball and a hoop! You can play by yourself to practice shooting and dribbling, or play one-on-one with a friend.

A football's oval shape and pointed ends make it easier to carry and throw.

Football players wear padding, face masks, and hard helmets to protect their bodies.

Football

It's called football, but in this sport players use their hands more than their feet! Two teams of 11 players take turns trying to throw or carry the football toward their opponent's end zone. When a player catches or carries the ball inside that end zone, their team scores. This is called a touchdown.

Each team gets four tries, called downs, to move the ball up the field at least 10 yards (9.1 m). If they do, they get four more tries and keep going. If they don't, they have to give the ball to the other team.

The seven officials on the field are nicknamed the "zebras" for their striped shirts. Their job is to make sure that players follow the rules.

If a player carrying the ball drops it, that's called a fumble. Either team can pick it up.

A football team has different squads, or groups, of players for offense and defense. The offense comes onto the field when their team has the ball. They run with or throw the ball to try to score. The defense comes onto the field when the other team has the ball. Their job is to stop the other team from scoring.

The best way to throw a football is with a spiral. This spins the ball so that one of its pointed ends is aimed at the target.

On defense, tacklers try to knock down whoever has the ball. On offense, blockers try to protect the player with the ball.

20

Two types of players do use their feet! Punters make long, high kicks to give the ball back to the other team. Placekickers score points by kicking the ball from the ground through the goalposts at the end of the field. They are part of a third squad of players called the special team, which comes on the field during kicking plays.

FLAG FOOTBALL

Flag football has many of the same rules as football, but there's no tackling. Players wear long streamers, or flags, that are attached to belts. A play ends when a player on the other team pulls off the ball carrier's flag.

The Football Field

END ZONE

GOALPOST

On offense, a player called the center "snaps," or quickly passes, the ball to the quarterback to start each play.

YARD LINES

Long lines on the field mark every 5 yards (4.8 m).

40 30 20 10 10 20 30 40 0

20 30 40 5

5 40 30 20

END ZONE
The end zone is 10 yards deep at each end of the field.

END ZONE

GET TO THE POINT

Touchdown . . . . **6 points**

Point After
Touchdown (PAT) . . . . . **1 or 2 points**
Teams get one point for kicking the ball over the crossbar and between the goalposts. They get two points if they carry or pass the ball into the end zone from the two-yard line.

Field Goal . . . . **3 points**
A kick that goes over the crossbar and between the goalposts. The ball can be kicked from anywhere on the field and on any down.

Safety . . . . **2 points**
When the defense tackles an offensive player in the offense's end zone.

Play stops when the ball goes beyond the sidelines.

LET'S PLAY!
Ready to practice some football skills? Set up a target on an outdoor wall, and try throwing the ball to hit it. Or set up some cones on the ground, and run in a zigzag between them while you carry the football.

0 40 30 20 10

SIDELINE

The catcher squats behind the batter at home plate. Catchers wear special helmets, face masks, and pads to protect their bodies.

FACTS

A baseball game is divided into nine periods called innings. When each team has batted once, one inning is complete.

After three batters are out, the teams trade places.

If a batter hits the ball and runs to all four bases in one play, that's called a home run.

People have been playing baseball for nearly 200 years.

Baseball

Batter up! This ball-and-bat sport is played around the world. There are two teams of nine players each. When one team is up at bat, the other team is on the field.

Some pitchers can throw a baseball faster than 100 miles an hour (161 km/h)!

The game begins when the pitcher throws the baseball to a batter at home plate. The batter tries to hit the ball and run around the four bases to score one point, called a run. Players on the field, called fielders, try to get the batter out by catching the ball before it hits the ground, tagging the batter with the ball, or tagging the base before the batter gets there. A batter can also "strike out" by failing to put the ball into play before the pitcher has thrown three fair pitches.

A batter can slide into a base to reach it before getting tagged out.

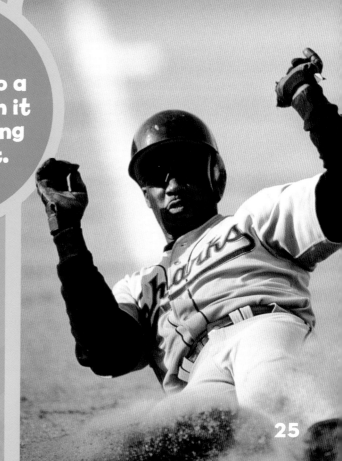

25

The Baseball Field

Bases are heavy and padded. Base runners can't be tagged out when they are touching a base.

Any ball that lands outside the foul lines is not in play.

FOUL LINE

LET'S PLAY!

Find a baseball diamond and practice your baserunning. Time each other to see who can run all the way around the bases the fastest.

OUTFIELD
The outfield is the area beyond the infield.

INFIELD
The infield includes the four bases and all the space between them.

PITCHER'S MOUND
A pitcher throws the ball from this raised area made of dirt.

The infield is called a baseball diamond. Can you guess why?

HOME PLATE
A batter stands here to hit the ball. It's also the last base a player must touch to score one point, or run.

The softballs used in games today are not really soft. They are nearly as hard as baseballs!

Most softball games are played to seven innings.

Softball

A softball field is smaller than a baseball field. But a softball is bigger than a baseball! These two sports are played in much the same way. Batters hit the ball and run the bases. Fielders catch and throw the ball to try to get the batter out.

Softball is played in two ways: fast-pitch and slow-pitch. The main difference is in how the pitcher throws the ball. Fast-pitch pitchers whirl their arms around and throw the ball underhand very quickly toward home plate. Slow-pitch pitchers throw the ball underhand in a high arc.

When first played, softball used a larger, squishier, softer ball, which is how the game got its name.

FACTS

A goal in soccer is worth one point.

The men's and women's World Cups match the best national teams against each other.

The World Cups are played every four years in a different country.

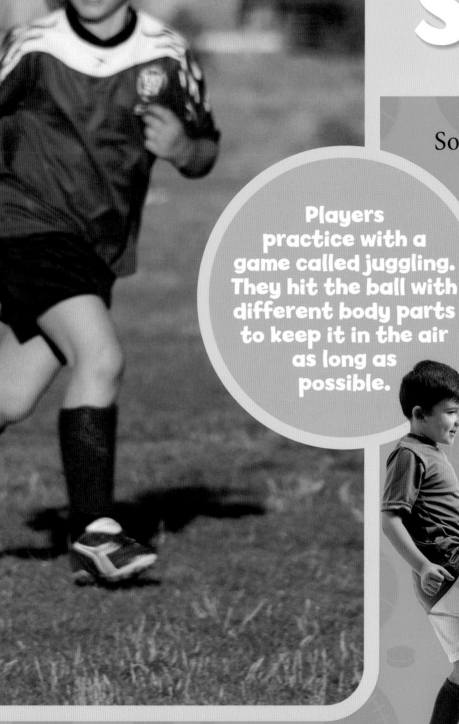

Soccer

Soccer is a fast-moving, back-and-forth game. More people play and watch soccer than any other sport in the world.

Two teams of 11 players move the ball around a large field with a goal at each end. Everyone but the goalie can touch the ball with any part of their body except their hands and arms. They try to get the ball into the other team's goal. The team that scores the most goals wins.

Players practice with a game called juggling. They hit the ball with different body parts to keep it in the air as long as possible.

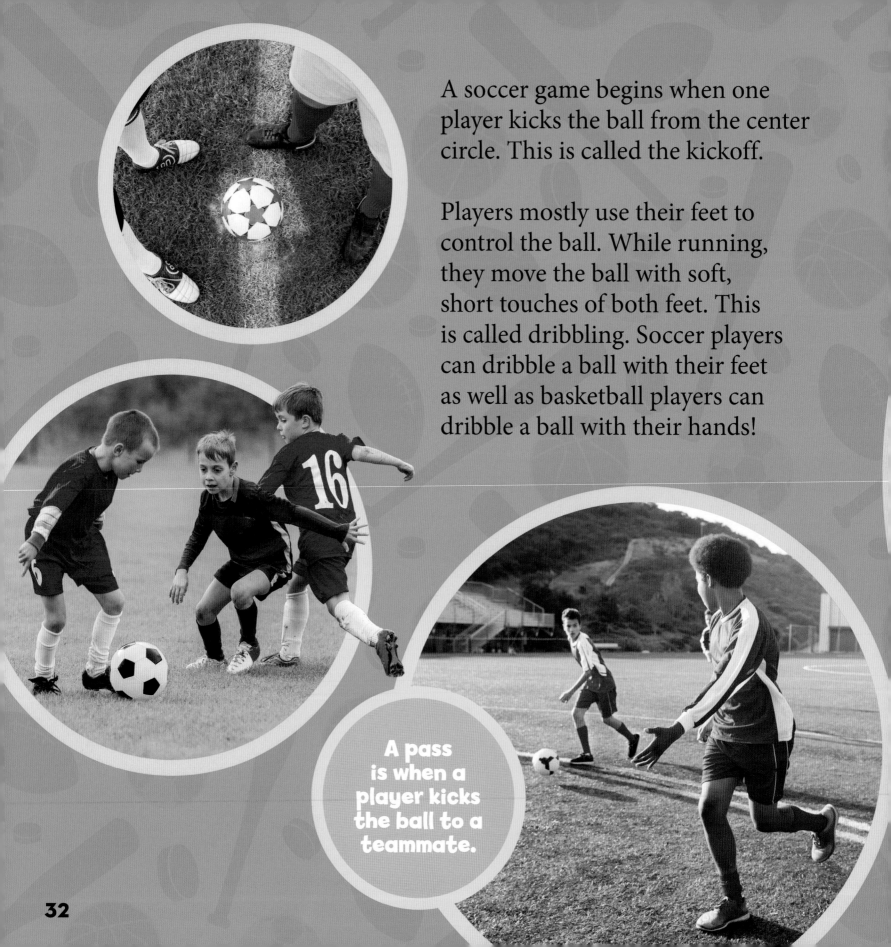

A soccer game begins when one player kicks the ball from the center circle. This is called the kickoff.

Players mostly use their feet to control the ball. While running, they move the ball with soft, short touches of both feet. This is called dribbling. Soccer players can dribble a ball with their feet as well as basketball players can dribble a ball with their hands!

A pass is when a player kicks the ball to a teammate.

The goalie tries to block the ball from entering the goal.

A shot is a kick directed toward the goal.

The Soccer Field

A soccer field is also called a pitch.

Fouls include tripping, pushing, or holding a player who has the ball.

A corner kick restarts play when the ball is kicked out of bounds.

PENALTY BOX

When a player commits a foul inside their own penalty area, a player from the team that was fouled takes a penalty kick inside the penalty box.

CORNER ARC

A flag marks each corner of the field. Corner kicks are taken from this small arc.

CENTER CIRCLE

Play starts from here at the beginning of each half and after each goal.

GOALPOST

A goal is scored when the ball fully crosses the line between the goalposts and under the crossbar.

LET'S PLAY!

The most important skill in soccer is controlling the ball. Ask a friend to throw or kick the ball to you. Practice stopping the ball with your feet. Try dribbling, moving the ball with quick, light touches.

35

Players are allowed to knock the puck down with their hand, but they cannot grab it unless they are a goalie.

Ice Hockey

Zoom! Ice hockey players skate fast on the ice! This sport began in Canada. It started as a fun way to play on frozen ponds and rivers.

Teams of six players skate on an ice sheet called a rink. The rink is shaped like a rectangle with rounded corners. They use sticks to move a hard rubber disk, called a puck, around the ice. Each team tries to hit the puck into their opponent's net.

Pond hockey is a kind of ice hockey played outdoors on frozen lakes and ponds.

FACTS

Professional ice hockey games last for 60 minutes. The games are broken into three 20-minute periods.

Four officials skate on the ice with the players to make sure they follow the rules.

Ice hockey is the national sport of Canada.

What do you like to play if the weather gets cold?

A goalie wears a catching glove and a face mask, too.

A face-off starts each hockey game. A referee drops the puck between one player from each team. Each player tries to quickly pass the puck to a teammate. The team without the puck tries to steal it or block passes.

Players wear thick pads and hard helmets to protect themselves.

In a slap shot, a player swings the stick up high and then sweeps it fast toward the puck.

Slap shots can travel more than 100 miles an hour (161 km/h).

Older players are allowed to smack into each other if they're trying to get the puck. This is called checking. Checking can knock over a player so that the opponent can steal the puck.

A goalie protects each goal. Goalies try to block fast-moving pucks from getting into the net.

STREET HOCKEY

You can play hockey without ice! In street hockey, players sometimes use a rubber ball instead of a puck. Players pass and shoot the ball at a goal protected by a goalie.

39

The Hockey Rink

BLUE LINE
This line divides the different zones in a rink.

FACE-OFF CIRCLE
An official drops the puck in one of these circles to restart play.

The crease is the area of blue paint in front of the goal. Players cannot touch the goalie when she is in the crease.

Stickhandling is when a player moves the puck quickly from one side of the stick's blade to the other.

THE BIG FIVE

CENTER CIRCLE

A face-off is held here to start each period and after each goal.

GOAL

A goal stands at each end of the rink. The puck is aimed here.

RED LINE

This marks the center of the rink.

LET'S PLAY!

No ice? No problem! Test your stickhandling skills on a course of cones set up on a basketball court or a playground. Try to keep a ball on your stick as you walk through the cones.

CHAPTER 2
Team Sports

All around the world, people gather to play sports on many kinds of fields. They kick, hit, and throw balls of all sizes. Here's a look at some more fun team sports!

Field Hockey

Thousands of years ago, people in ancient Greece played a game that was kind of like field hockey. Today field hockey is played with teams of 11.

Players use sticks to move a hard ball across a rectangular field. A goal stands at either end of the field.

Players swing their sticks to pass the ball along the ground to a teammate or to shoot the ball into the goal. The team without the ball tries to block or steal passes. Each team's goalkeeper tries to block the ball from going into the net.

SHOOTING CIRCLE

Goals can only be scored from inside an area called the shooting circle.

44

Players can hit the ball only with the flat side of the stick.

How do you think field hockey is different from ice hockey?

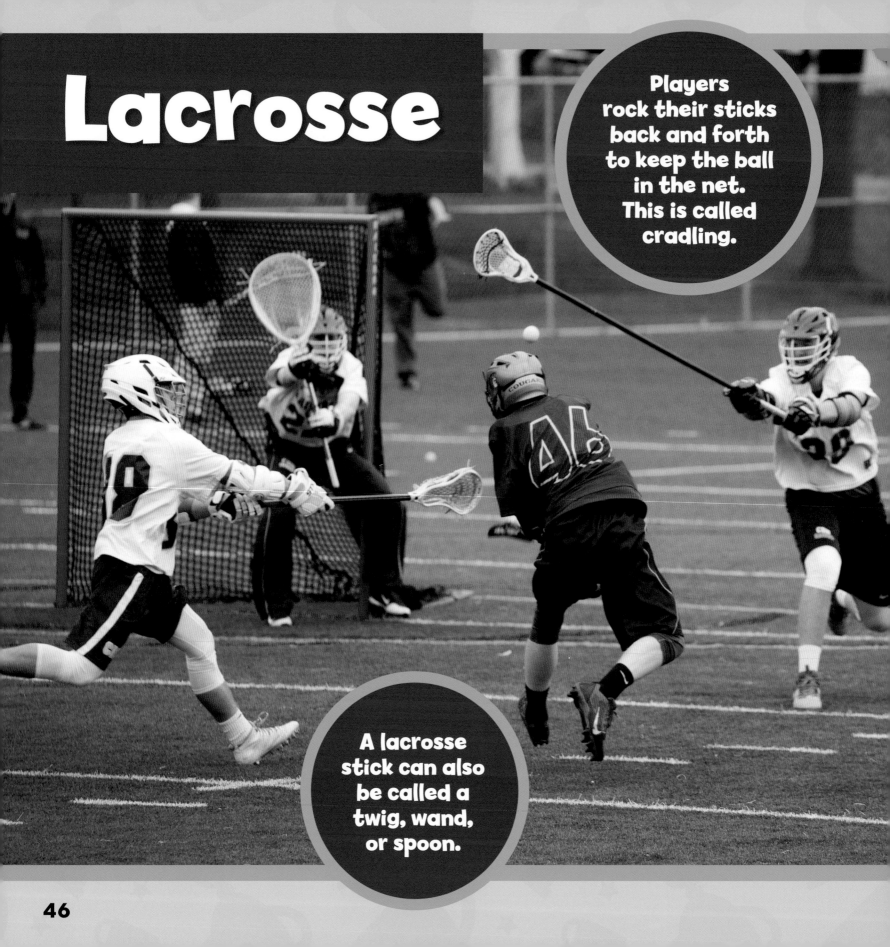

Lacrosse

Players rock their sticks back and forth to keep the ball in the net. This is called cradling.

A lacrosse stick can also be called a twig, wand, or spoon.

FACTS

A goal is worth one point.

The goal is surrounded by a circular area called the crease. A player cannot step inside this area to score.

The goalie's stick has a larger net than the other players' sticks.

Box lacrosse is an indoor version of the sport.

The Native American Algonquin tribe called this game baggataway. The game was sometimes played over several miles! And a baggataway game could last for days.

Today, lacrosse is played on a field by two teams of 10 or 12 players. Players each use a stick with a small net at the end to catch, carry, and pass the ball. They try to fling the ball into their opponent's goal. Each team has a goalie who protects their team's goal.

Cheerleading

"1, 2, 3, 4! Let me hear you stomp the floor!" Cheerleaders yell and shout to get a crowd excited about a game.

This sport combines dance and gymnastics. Cheerleaders also perform stunts together. In the basket toss, two people called the bases hold each other's arms to form a "basket." They toss one person, called the flyer, into the air and then catch them in the basket. "Go, team!"

FACTS

Cheerleading began about 150 years ago.

Cheerleaders were first called yell leaders.

Cheerleading is also called cheer.

A mount is when one or more cheerleaders are held up in the air. It's also called a stunt.

A herkie is a cheerleading jump.

A high V is when both arms are raised in the air to form a V shape.

Would you rather be a base or a flyer in a cheerleading stunt?

A rugby ball is thicker and longer than an American football.

Rugby

Two teams play rugby on a large grass field with a goal area at each end. Players move an oval-shaped ball around by passing it, kicking it, or running with it. They can only pass the ball backward.

When one team has the ball, the other team tries to take it away by tackling the ballcarrier. Points are scored when a player carries the ball into the goal area or kicks it over a crossbar at either end of the field.

In a scrum, players from both teams link their arms together and try to kick the ball out of the circle.

FACTS

Teams can have seven, 13, or 15 players, depending on the type of rugby played.

Tackles are not allowed above the shoulders or below the knees.

Rugby is named for the school in England where the sport was first played.

Cricket

This is a sport, not an insect!
Two teams of 11 play
on an oval grass field.
A long dirt rectangle
called the pitch runs
down the center of
the field.

At each end of the pitch
is a set of three sticks
called a wicket. These are
topped by two smaller sticks called bails.
A player called a bowler stands at one
end of the pitch and throws a small,
hard ball toward a batter at the other
end. When the bowler throws the ball
past the batter and knocks the bails
off the wicket, the batter is out. But if
the batter hits the ball and runs back and
forth between the two wickets, he scores a run
for his team.

The wicketkeeper's job is to catch balls that the batter doesn't hit.

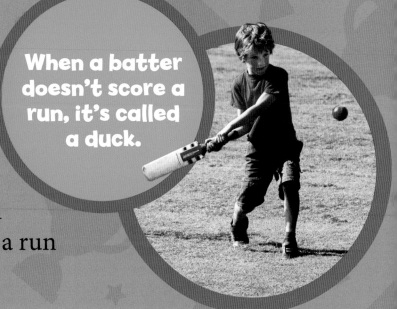

When a batter doesn't score a run, it's called a duck.

Bowlers must keep their arm straight when they throw the ball; they can't bend their elbow.

FACTS

Cricket is very popular in England, India, Pakistan, South Africa, and Australia.

If the batter hits the ball and the other team catches it before it hits the ground, the batter is out.

A ball that is hit to the edge of the field is worth four runs, or points. A ball that goes outside the oval boundary is worth six points.

53

Ultimate

Ultimate players often leap or dive to catch the disc.

Students at a high school in New Jersey, U.S.A., first played this game.

FACTS

Ultimate players sometimes do "rock-paper-scissors" to determine which team gets the disc first.

A player can throw the disc in any direction to a teammate.

Most games don't have referees. Players make the calls themselves.

What do you get when you combine football, basketball, and a plastic flying disc with a little gymnastics? A sport called ultimate!

Two teams of seven players throw a disc to their teammates on a big field. A team scores a point when a player catches the disc in their opponent's end zone.

The team without the disc plays defense. Players can try to block a pass, but they cannot touch their opponents. If a player drops the disc, the other team picks it up. The team with the most points at the end of the game wins.

Players cannot walk or run while holding the disc.

Have you ever thrown a flying disc around?

FACTS

The first team to get to 25 points wins the game.

The same player cannot hit the ball twice in a row.

Players cannot catch, hold, or throw the ball.

"Volley" means to hit a ball in the air before it lands on the ground.

BUMP

Volleyball

Bump, set, spike! In volleyball, two teams of six players hit a ball back and forth over a net that stands in the center of a rectangular court. The game starts with a serve, a single hit of the ball over the net. The team that is receiving the ball has up to three hits to knock it back over the net.

SPIKE

The first hit is called a bump or a dig. A player uses their forearms to hit the ball. The second hit is usually the set. A player uses their hands to make an overhead pass to a teammate. The third hit is often a spike. A player uses one open hand to hit the ball hard and fast toward the ground on the other side of the net. If the team receiving the ball can't return it, the other team scores a point.

SET

Playground Sports

KICKBALL

A pitcher rolls a bouncy ball toward the kicker. After kicking the ball, the kicker tries to run around the bases and make it to home base without getting tagged. The team that scores the most runs wins.

KABADDI

Hold your breath and try to make it past a line of players. If you get tagged or breathe, you're out!

DOUBLE DUTCH

Two people spin two jump ropes at once, and one or more people hop over the ropes.

FOUR SQUARE

On a grid of four connected squares, four players bounce a ball to each other with their hands. A player is out if they hit the ball out of bounds or miss the ball.

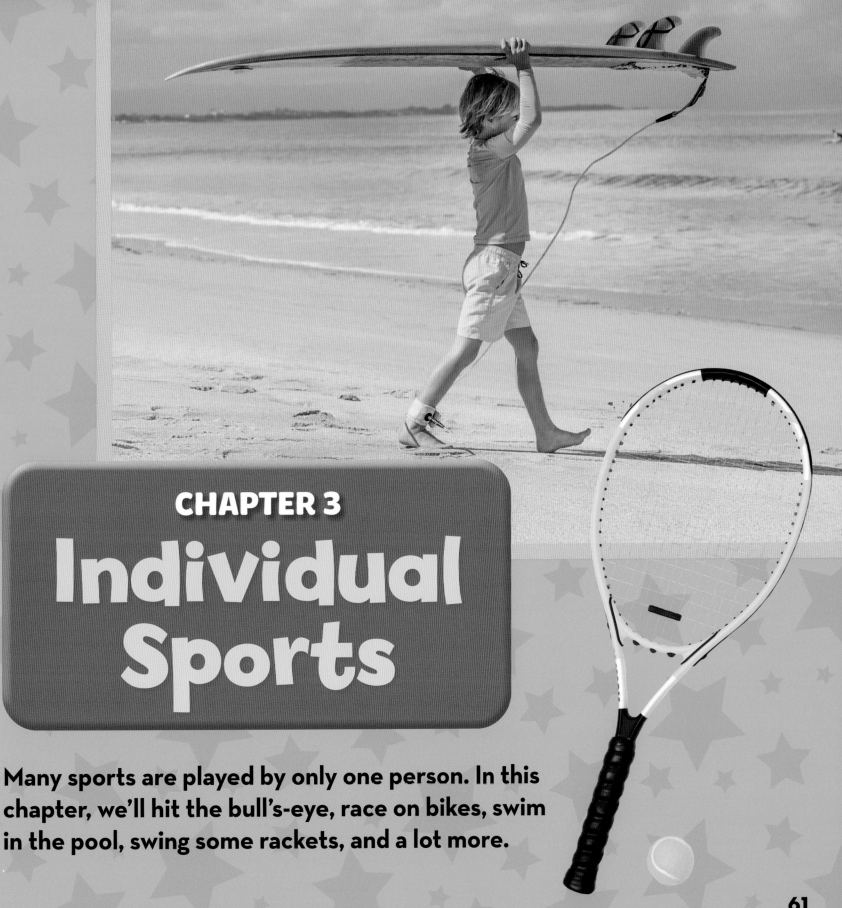

CHAPTER 3
Individual Sports

Many sports are played by only one person. In this chapter, we'll hit the bull's-eye, race on bikes, swim in the pool, swing some rackets, and a lot more.

Archery

FACTS

The part at the back of the arrow is called the fletching. It helps steer the arrow as it flies through the air.

The straight part of the arrow is called the shaft.

The bag that archers use to hold their arrows is called a quiver.

A peeker is an archer who aims the bow and then lowers it to look at the target again.

A "Robin Hood" is when an archer splits an arrow down its center by firing another arrow into it.

This is one of the oldest sports in this book! Humans created the bow and arrow more than 60,000 years ago to hunt for food. Today, the sport of archery uses the same technique. Archers put an arrow in the bow, pull back the bowstring, aim for the target, and release the arrow.

Archers aim their arrow at a target that has 10 rings. Each ring is worth a different number of points. The ring in the center, called the bull's-eye, is worth 10 points.

Hold out a thumbtack as far as you can. That tack is how small the bull's-eye looks to an Olympic archer!

Can you pretend to aim an arrow at a target? Try it!

Bowling

About 650 years ago, soldiers in England enjoyed rolling a ball to try to knock over objects. The king thought they played the game, called bowling, too much. He told them they couldn't play it anymore!

Bowling is still popular today. Players use one hand to hold a heavy bowling ball. Bowlers aim at 10 large pins that are arranged in a triangle at the end of a narrow wooden lane. The goal is to knock down as many pins as they can with each roll, or throw.

After two throws, which together are called a frame, all 10 pins are set up again. Ten frames make up a game.

Scientists discovered an ancient Egyptian hallway that they think was an indoor bowling alley!

FACTS

A strike is when a player knocks down all 10 pins with one throw.

A spare is when a player knocks down all 10 pins with two throws.

A turkey is when a player gets three strikes in a row.

A gutter ball is when the ball lands in the gutter on either side of the lane.

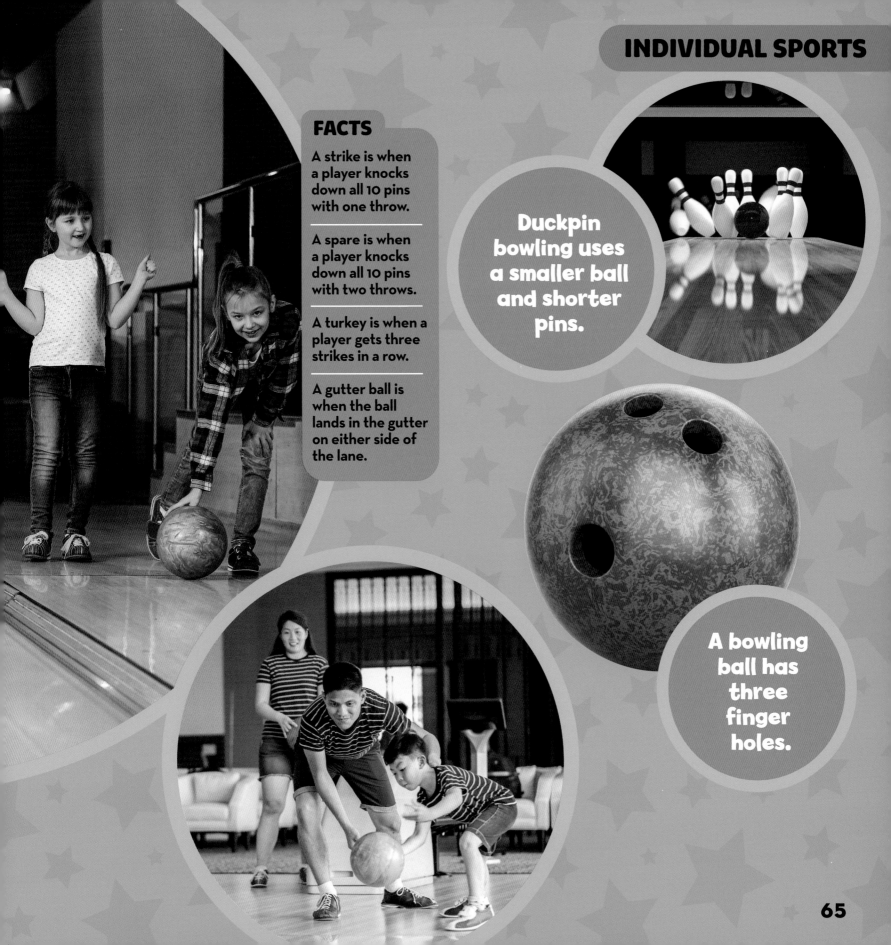

Duckpin bowling uses a smaller ball and shorter pins.

A bowling ball has three finger holes.

To form a bridge, a wrestler moves his body into a bridge-like shape to try to avoid getting pinned to the mat.

Wrestling

FACTS

Wrestlers are placed in different groups, or classes, based on how much they weigh.

In a whizzer, a wrestler puts his arm around an opponent's arm and body to prevent him from moving.

A referee makes sure wrestlers follow the rules so that everyone stays safe.

Wrestling is another sport that has been around for a long time. Cave paintings from prehistoric times show people in wrestling poses. Artwork from ancient Egypt shows wrestlers using some of the same moves seen in the sport today.

Wrestling was part of the earliest Olympic Games in ancient Greece.

Wrestling matches are held on large padded mats. The match begins when two wrestlers stand up and face each other. They use their arms and legs to try to pin their opponent to the mat. They get points for certain moves or throws.

Cycling

ADAPTIVE BIKE

Ever since bicycles were invented, people have wanted to race them! The sport of cycling quickly became popular around the world.

Today, there are many different types of cycling. Road cycling takes place outside on paved streets. In track cycling, cyclists speed around a circular indoor track called a velodrome. Mountain bikers ride outdoors on bumpy and twisty dirt tracks. But indoors or outdoors, the person who crosses the finish line first wins!

In bicycle motocross, or BMX, cyclists race on a dirt track with jumps and sharp turns.

The first bicycle, invented in 1817, didn't have pedals! Riders used their feet to move forward.

Which type of cycling sounds like the most fun?

TOUR DE FRANCE

The world's most famous cycling race is held each year in France. It lasts for about a month and covers about 2,200 miles (3,500 km). Cyclists ride a certain distance each day. Some of the roads are flat. Others go over steep mountains.

69

Fencers salute each other at the start of a game. Then the referee calls out "On guard!"

Fencing

Fencers wear jackets with sensors that record each touch. Lights go on and fencers hear a beep when a point is scored.

Long ago, soldiers trained for battle by practicing with swords that did not hurt their opponents. The sport called fencing grew out of this.

Today, a fencing match takes place on a mat called a strip. Fencers try to touch each other with the tip of their swords. They use their swords to block their opponent, too. The fencer who scores the highest number of touches on her opponent is the winner.

ÉPÉE

SABRE

The three types of fencing swords are épée, foil, and sabre.

FOIL

71

A hole in one is when a golfer hits the ball from the tee into the hole with only one stroke.

FAIRWAY
This is a long strip of short grass.

The green is an area of short grass where the hole is located.

TEE
This short peg raises the ball off the ground.

Golf

Golf as it is played today started more than 500 years ago. Some stories say that as shepherds watched their flocks, they used their long staffs to whack rocks on the ground. Over time, this turned into an organized game. Special sticks called clubs replaced the staffs. Golf balls were used instead of rocks.

Today, golfers play on special courses. They use different types of clubs to hit the golf ball from the tee to the green. The goal is to get the ball into the hole on the green in as few hits, or strokes, as possible. Most golf matches cover 18 holes. The lowest score wins!

DRIVER

WOOD

IRON

PUTTER

TYPES OF GOLF CLUBS

Driver: Used to hit the first, longest tee shot

Wood: Used for long shots after the tee shot

Iron: Used for shorter shots

Putter: Used to roll the ball on the green

Most tennis balls are yellow, which makes them easy to see.

FACTS

A score of zero in tennis is called "love."

A tie score in a tennis game is called "deuce."

Tennis rackets today are usually made of graphite.

A rally is when the players hit the ball back and forth over the net.

Tennis

Professional players can serve the ball faster than 100 miles an hour (161 km/h).

People used their bare hands to play an early form of this game! They hit a small wooden ball over a rope or net. Later, a wooden racket with strings took the place of a player's open palms. This game became known as tennis.

In doubles tennis, teams of two play each other.

Today, tennis is played on courts made of grass, clay, or a hard surface. One player stands on each side of a net that runs across the center of the court. A point begins when one player serves the ball. They toss the ball into the air and hit it with their racket. If their opponent doesn't hit the ball back over the net or hits it outside the lines on the court, the person who served gets a point.

What do you think the outside of a tennis ball feels like?

More Racket Sports

TABLE TENNIS

This sport is also called Ping-Pong because of the sound the ball makes when it hits the paddle.

PICKLEBALL
This sport is a kind of tennis played with shorter rackets on a smaller court.

SQUASH
The name comes from the soft or "squashy" ball that's hit with a racket against the four walls of the court.

What is your favorite game to play outdoors?

BADMINTON
A lightweight shuttlecock, or birdie, is hit with a racket on a court with a high net.

In sport climbing, competitors race to see who can make it to the top of the wall first.

Rock Climbing

You don't need rocks to do this sport! On an indoor or outdoor climbing wall, climbers use their hands and feet to grab and step on plastic knobs to reach the top. They keep three touch points on the wall at all times. They grip the surface with two feet and a hand or finger.

The same form is used on a steep cliff or mountainside. Rock climbers look for tiny bumps or cracks where they can place their fingers and toes. Then they use their arms and legs to pull themselves up.

Most climbers wear special shoes with sticky rubber soles.

Rock climbers carry a small bag with powdery chalk inside. They put it on their hands to get a better grip on the rock.

What do you like to climb?

79

Athletes do spins while holding on to a pair of rings above the ground.

To keep from slipping, gymnasts use chalk on their hands.

Gymnastics

This sport can make you say, "Wow! How do they do that?" Gymnasts use different types of gear, or just their bodies, to perform amazing feats of strength, balance, grace, and style.

In competitions, gymnasts perform in many different events. Some of these are shown here. Judges award points to each gymnast based on how hard a move is and how well the gymnast performs it.

Gymnasts bounce high off the vault, flipping and twisting in the air before landing.

On the balance beam, gymnasts flip, leap, cartwheel, and turn.

Before a karate match begins, competitors bow to each other as a sign of respect.

Karate

Tae kwon do, judo, hapkido, jiujitsu, and kung fu are other kinds of martial arts.

This Japanese martial art, or combat sport, has not changed since it was first taught hundreds of years ago. Two people use their hands, arms, and legs to strike, block, and kick each other. The goal is not to hurt your opponent but to show focus, control, correct form, and good sportsmanship.

Students earn different colored belts as their skills improve. A beginner wears a white belt. A black belt is the highest level. The levels in between have yellow, orange, green, blue, purple, brown, and red belts.

JUDO

What's your favorite color?

In kata karate, athletes perform movements by themselves, without an opponent.

Surfing

Surf's up! The first surfers probably lived on islands in the South Pacific Ocean. They rode the waves on wooden boards. Over the years, surfing became a worldwide sport.

Today, surfers ride the waves on hard boards. To start, a surfer lies on the board and uses their arms to paddle far out from the shore. Then they sit up. When they see a wave they like, they quickly point the board toward the beach and stand up. The speeding wave catches the surfboard, and the ride begins!

Fins on the bottom of a surfboard help it go straight.

In surfing competitions, riders catch waves and do tricks while judges watch and award points. There are even competitions for dogs!

84

A rubber leash on the board attaches to the surfer's ankle so she doesn't lose her board in the water.

TALK THE TALK

Surfing has a cool language all its own. How many of these words have you heard?

Barrel: the tube-shaped part of a wave

Grom: short for grommet, a new surfer

Hang ten: ride with both feet at the front end of the board

Nug: short for nugget, a great wave to ride

Stoked: very happy

Wipeout: falling off the board during a ride

In a race in a pool, each swimmer must stay in a lane marked by floating ropes.

Many swimmers wear goggles to keep water out of their eyes and swim caps to hold their hair out of the way.

86

Swimming and Diving

Everybody into the pool! Swimming is a fun way to spend time with your family and friends, but it's also a sport. Athletes of every age take part in swim meets around the world.

Swimmers compete in races of different lengths. There are four types of styles, or strokes: front crawl, breaststroke, butterfly, and backstroke. Each stroke uses different arm and leg motions.

Diving is another sport done in pools. Divers leap into the water from a bouncy springboard or hard platform. On the way down, they spin, twist, flip, and somersault. Judges award them points based on how well they perform their dive.

What's your favorite place to go swimming?

More Water Sports

STAND-UP PADDLEBOARDING

A rider balances on a board and uses a paddle to move through the water.

ROWING

A rower uses oars to race a boat, called a shell, through the water.

SAILING

Sailors steer boats by moving the sails to catch the wind.

Skateboarding

Skateboarding was invented by some surfers in California, U.S.A. They wanted something to ride when the ocean's waves were flat. They attached roller-skate wheels to the bottom of small wooden boards. They used their feet to push off from the ground. This land surfing caught on.

In skateboarding competitions, skaters perform for judges who award points. In street and park competitions, skaters roll through a series of obstacles and perform tricks. In a vert competition, skaters zoom back and forth on ramps. In Big Air, skaters see who can go the highest and perform the trickiest jumps above a ramp.

To "get air" is to ride with all four wheels off the ground.

A "grab" is when the skater uses their hand (or hands) to hold the board during a trick.

The deck is the flat surface of the skateboard. The nose is the front of the skateboard, and the tail is the rear.

Which skateboarding competition would you most like to do?

91

Track and Field

On your mark, get set, go! Running a race is one of the world's oldest sports. At the first recorded Olympic Games in ancient Greece, in 776 B.C., there was only one event: a short footrace.

Today's track events include running and walking. Races are held on a flat, oval track. Races are run at many different distances. Each racer starts in a lane that is marked by painted lines.

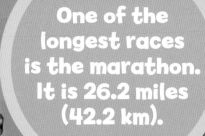

One of the longest races is the marathon. It is 26.2 miles (42.2 km).

In one kind of track event, runners leap over hurdles.

The events that make up track and field are also called "athletics."

Field events include forms of jumping and throwing. Pole vaulters use a long pole to push themselves up and over a high bar. In the high jump, athletes leap over a tall bar. Long jumpers run up to a board and then leap forward into a pit filled with sand.

LONG JUMP

JAVELIN

Pole vaulters and high jumpers land on thick padded mats after their leaps.

Field athletes also throw different types of objects. A javelin is a long, thin spear. The shot put is an iron ball. The discus is a flat disc. Athletes also throw the hammer, a heavy ball at the end of a long wire that they swing around their head many times before releasing it into the air.

Most high jumpers jump over the bar backward.

POLE VAULT

SHOT PUT

Motorsports

MOTORCYCLE
Riders balance around tight curves as they race on a flat course.

NASCAR
Drivers race cars called stock cars around an oval track.

INDYCAR
Drivers steer cars called open-wheel racers around an oval or twisting track.

MOTOCROSS
Motorcyclists race on dirt tracks with hills and sharp turns.

FORMULA 1
High-tech machines battle in the world's most popular motorsport.

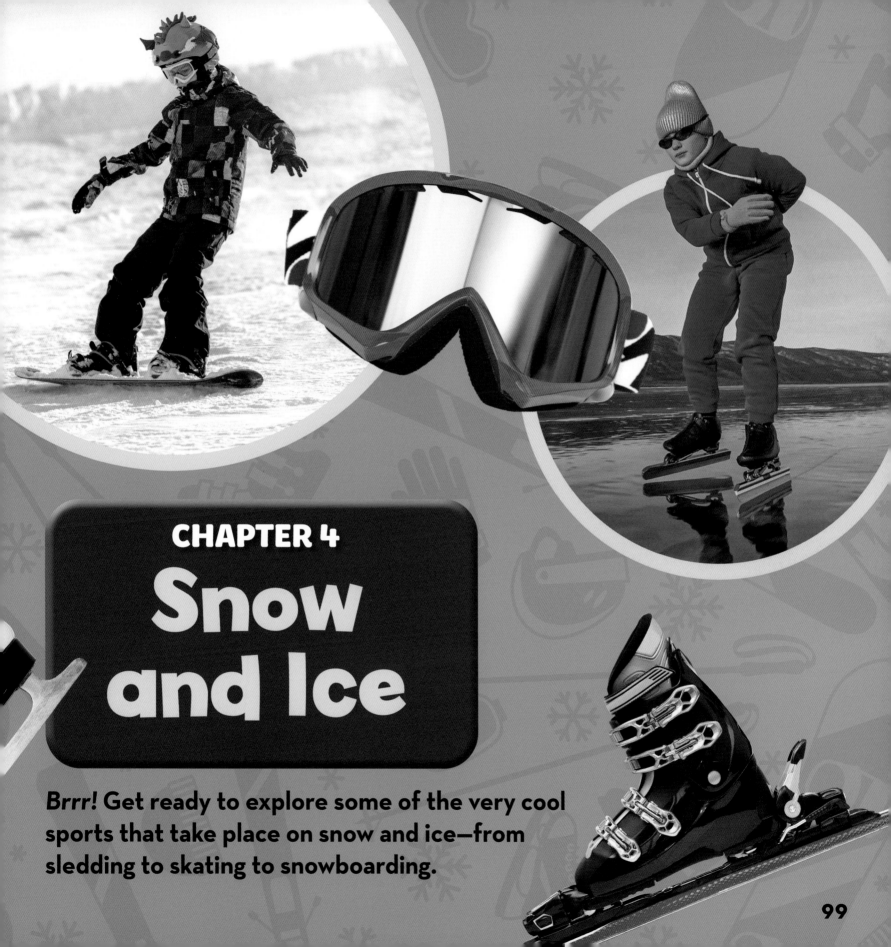

CHAPTER 4
Snow and Ice

Brrr! Get ready to explore some of the very cool sports that take place on snow and ice—from sledding to skating to snowboarding.

FACTS

A curling stone weighs about as much as a seven-year-old child!

Each team slides up to 80 stones in a game.

A skip, or captain, leads a curling team and directs its plays.

Curling is sometimes called the "roaring game" because the stone makes a rumbling sound as it slides across the ice.

Curling

Hundreds of years ago in Scotland, people gathered on frozen ponds to play a fun wintertime game. They pushed large, smooth stones on the icy surface to see whose stone hit a target first. Over time this activity, called curling, spread to other parts of Europe and North America.

In a curling match today, two teams of four take turns sliding stones topped with a handle along a long strip, or sheet, of ice. They aim for the "house," a target painted on the other end of the sheet. The team that gets their stone closest to the center, or button, of the house wins.

Curlers use "brooms" to sweep the ice in front of the stone. This helps the stone move farther and keeps it from "curling," or changing direction.

Have you ever seen a pond or lake frozen over with ice?

Today's ice skates have thin, sharp blades, but early ice skates were flat on the bottom.

In pairs ice skating, two skaters perform a routine that includes lifts and throws.

Figure skating is a popular sport wherever there are indoor ice rinks, not just in cold places!

Figure Skating

The first ice skates were used almost 4,000 years ago. They were made out of animal bone. People skated to get from one place to another when waterways froze in the wintertime.

In the 1800s, steel skate blades were invented. These helped skaters turn and move more easily across ice. An American ballet dancer then created dance-like movements for ice skating.

In figure skating competitions today, skaters spin, twirl, and jump on an oval rink of ice. These moves are part of a routine that is set to music. Judges award points for a skater's skill, balance, and style.

Ice skates have a toe pick at the front of each blade. These sawlike ridges allow skaters to push off from the ice and jump into the air.

Can you balance on one leg like this skater? Try it!

Speed Skating

In some parts of the Netherlands, kids can skate to school.

FACTS

Most speed skating races are held between two skaters on a two-lane track.

In short-track speed skating, four to six skaters compete on a smaller track with no lanes.

A breakaway is when one speed skater gains a big lead over the other in a race.

Speed skating is ice skating—fast! The best speed skaters can go faster than 30 miles an hour (48 km/h).

The first speed skating races were held on frozen lakes and rivers. With swinging arms and strong legs, today's speed skaters whip around an oval ice track. The first skater to cross the finish line is the winner.

Speed skate boots have longer blades than ice skates.

Skiing

People have been using skis to travel across snow for at least 8,000 years! The first skis were made of heavy pieces of wood. Over time, skis became thinner, lighter, and easier to use. And skiing became a popular sport around the world.

In alpine skiing, skiers zip down steep hills. Nordic, or cross-country, skiers compete on flatter areas of snow. They take long strides and move each ski forward, one at a time. In both kinds of skiing, the fastest skier wins.

Freestyle skiers go down hills that have big bumps, ramps, and other obstacles. They jump into the air and perform flips and spins.

Skiers carry two poles to help them balance. They also wear goggles and a helmet for protection.

"Ski" comes from a Norwegian word that means "stick of wood."

In the downhill event called the slalom, athletes ski around tall poles called gates.

107

Snowboarding

What do you call surfing on the snow? Snowboarding! On Christmas Day, 1965, a man named Sherman Poppen nailed two skis together. His two daughters then took turns sliding down their backyard hill on the board. The Snurfer, as Poppen called his snow surfboard, was an early form of today's snowboard.

One event in snowboarding competitions is called the half-pipe. Snowboarders slide up and down a smooth U-shaped track that is built out of snow. They do flips and other tricks in the air. Snowboarders also compete in downhill races.

TALK THE TALK

Here are the names of some awesome snowboard moves.

- Flying Squirrel Air
- Indy Grab
- Mosquito Air
- Nose Press
- Nuclear Air
- Phillips 66
- Rodeo Flip
- Stale Fish Air

A rider's feet face the side of the board, not the front.

HALF-PIPE

BINDING

Bindings attach the rider's boots to the board. They help snowboarders to better control the board.

Skeleton racers can go faster than a car on a highway.

Sledding

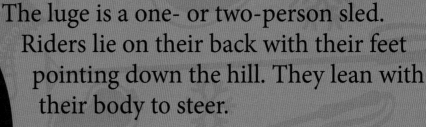

Sledding started as a way to move and carry things in the snow. Later on, blades called runners were added to the bottom of sleds. That made the sleds move faster. Soon people were racing sleds along an icy track. Today, there are three main kinds of sledding sports: bobsled, luge, and skeleton.

In bobsledding, one, two, or four people sit in a tube-shaped bobsled and steer down a narrow and twisty track.

Bobsledders run alongside the sled to push it into motion. Then they hop in and zip down the track.

LUGE

The luge is a one- or two-person sled. Riders lie on their back with their feet pointing down the hill. They lean with their body to steer.

Riders lie facedown on a skeleton sled. They hold their head up to see where they are going.

111

CHAPTER 5
The Olympics

The Olympic Games are the biggest sports event in the world. They began thousands of years ago in ancient Greece.

Summer Olympics

The first modern Olympics took place in Athens, Greece, in 1896. The Summer Games are normally held once every four years. Athletes from across the globe compete in sports like gymnastics, swimming, archery, track and field, soccer, volleyball, and basketball. The games are held in a different city each time.

Athletes earn a gold medal for first place, silver for second, and bronze for third.

The Olympic symbol is also called the Olympic rings. It stands for how athletes from five continents across the world come together to compete.

LET THE GAMES BEGIN

The Olympic Games begin with an opening ceremony. All the athletes parade into a stadium. Athletes from Greece lead the parade. Teams from other countries follow in alphabetical order. The team whose country is hosting the Olympics enters last. Fans cheer, flags wave, and everyone watches a show with music, dancing, and fireworks.

Winter Olympics

The first Winter Olympics were held in 1924 in France. Like the Summer Olympics, this event normally takes place every four years. Athletes gather to compete in sports played on snow and ice. These include figure skating, skiing, bobsledding, and ice hockey.

THE TORCH

The Olympic torch is a tradition of both the Summer and Winter Games. A flame is lit in Olympia, Greece. The flame is then passed from torch to torch on a relay that goes through many different countries. The relay lasts for weeks. The final torch lights a huge flame at the opening ceremony that glows throughout the games.

Paralympics

The Paralympics are held at the same time as the Summer and Winter Games. Many of the same events are included, but some of the sports equipment is adapted so that people with physical challenges can compete. Skis are built for sitting down instead of standing up, for example. And wheelchairs are used to race around a track or move a basketball down the court.

GOALBALL
This Olympic sport is played by athletes who are blind or vision impaired. The object of the game is to throw a ball into the other team's net to score points. The ball has bells inside so that athletes can hear it.

Special Olympics

The Special Olympics are for athletes age eight and older who have intellectual disabilities. Intellectual disabilities can cause a person to learn more slowly than other people the same age.

In Special Olympics events, athletes of all abilities compete in Olympic-style sports. These include bocce, cycling, skiing, gymnastics, powerlifting, swimming, sailing, and more.

Special Olympics competitions are held all around the world. There are thousands of events every year!

Which of these sports would you like to try?

EVEN MORE SPORTS

Here are a few more sports from around the world.

Fairbanks, Alaska (United States)

NORTH AMERICA

The World Eskimo-Indian Olympics are held each year in Fairbanks, Alaska, U.S.A. Events include the greased pole walk and knuckle hop (racers can move forward only on their knuckles and toes). In the western United States, rodeo includes bronco riding, barrel racing, and bareback riding.

PACIFIC OCEAN

NORTH AMERICA

United States

EUROPE

Jai alai is popular in Spain. Players wear long gloves with curved baskets on the end to catch and throw a ball on a narrow court. In Scotland, the Highland Games have taken place for centuries. In the caber toss, athletes try to flip a huge log with their bare hands.

Brazil

SOUTH AMERICA

ATLANTIC OCEAN

SOUTH AMERICA

Capoeira is a kind of martial art that is popular in Brazil. But unlike most martial arts, there is little or no contact between participants. It's as much a dance as it is a competition.

SOUTHERN OCEAN

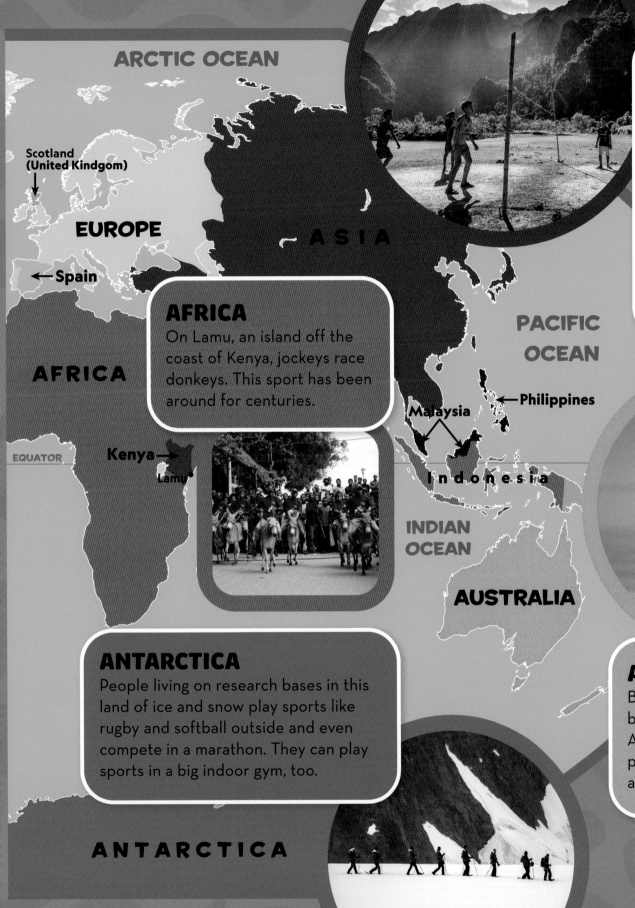

ARCTIC OCEAN

EUROPE

Scotland
(United Kindgom)

← Spain

ASIA

ASIA
Sepak Takraw is a game in which players leap to kick a small ball back and forth over a high net. It's popular in Indonesia, Malaysia, Thailand, the Philippines, and other parts of Southeast Asia.

AFRICA
On Lamu, an island off the coast of Kenya, jockeys race donkeys. This sport has been around for centuries.

AFRICA

PACIFIC OCEAN

Philippines

Malaysia

EQUATOR

Kenya →

Lamu

Indonesia

INDIAN OCEAN

AUSTRALIA

ANTARCTICA
People living on research bases in this land of ice and snow play sports like rugby and softball outside and even compete in a marathon. They can play sports in a big indoor gym, too.

AUSTRALIA
Boomerangs were first used by Australia's Indigenous Aboriginal people. Today, people throw them for fun, at targets, or for distance.

ANTARCTICA

PARENT TIPS

Extend your child's experience beyond the pages of this book. It's time to get out and play! Being active is a big part of staying healthy, and sports are a great way to do that. There are a lot of ways that kids can participate in organized sports, but they don't need a league or a coach or a uniform to have fun playing games and sports. Encourage your child to try some of the sports in this book. Here are some other sports-related activities you can do with National Geographic's *Little Kids First Big Book of Sports*.

INVENT A SPORT

After reading about all the sports in this book, why not make up a new one? See if your child can come up with a new type of race or a new way to play with a ball. Help him make up some rules so that everyone knows what to do. Then head out to the park (or the field or the gym or the pool) and play!

TRY SOMETHING NEW

Use the variety of sports in this book to see if your child wants to try something new. Talk about how exciting a new challenge can be. Read the rules of a particular sport together and then put them into practice, or find a local team and jump in!

WATCH AND LEARN

Pick a sports event on-screen and watch it with your child. Look closely at how the game is played and help her learn how to follow the score. If it's a team sport, pick one player and follow that player throughout the game. Then look at how the team interacts together. Talk with your child about how the athletes celebrated a win or responded to a disappointing play or loss.

GO TO A GAME

Live sports events are a great way to learn more about a sport. Whether it's a high school soccer game or a Little League baseball team or a college lacrosse squad, you can find a lot of sports in action almost anywhere you live.

MAKE A COLLAGE

Grab some old magazines and newspapers and make a sports collage. Help your child cut out pictures of her favorite sports and create an action-packed poster to hang on her wall. Cut out letters to make words that will cheer on her paper players!

LEARN SPORTS HISTORY

Sports has played a big part in world history. Head to the library, check out some sports history books, and help your child find out more. How did the Olympics begin? How did American football become so popular? How has the role of women in sports changed in the last few decades?

GLOSSARY

BOWLER: in cricket, the person who throws the ball toward the batter; in bowling, anyone who rolls the ball

DRIBBLING: in basketball, bouncing the ball with one hand; in soccer, controlling the ball using small kicks

END ZONE: the place on the field where a touchdown is scored in football

FREE THROW: in basketball, a shot given to a team that has been fouled

INNING: when three outs are made by each team in baseball

LOVE: a score of zero in tennis

PIN: in wrestling, to hold your opponent's back to the mat; in bowling, the objects at which the bowler aims

PUCK: the round, flat-sided disc that's hit in hockey

PUTTER: in golf, the flat-sided club used to hit the ball on the green

REBOUND: to grab a missed basketball shot

RINK: the ice sheet used in hockey, curling, and figure skating

SPIKE: a hard hit of a volleyball aimed at the opponent's side

SPRINGBOARD: a diving board on which divers can bounce up and down

STRIKE: in baseball, a pitch that goes through the strike zone; in bowling, knocking down all 10 pins at once

VELODROME: a banked indoor cycling track

WICKETS: in cricket, the three wooden sticks at each end of the center of the field

ADDITIONAL RESOURCES

BOOKS

Buckley, James, Jr. *It's a Numbers Game! Baseball.* National Geographic Kids Books, 2021.

Buckley, James, Jr. *It's a Numbers Game! Basketball.* National Geographic Kids Books, 2020.

Buckley, James, Jr. *It's a Numbers Game! Soccer.* National Geographic Kids Books, 2020.

Flynn, Sarah. *National Geographic Readers: Gymnastics.* National Geographic Kids Books, 2021.

Weird But True! Sports. National Geographic Kids Books, 2016.

Zweig, Eric. *Everything Sports.* National Geographic Kids Books, 2016.

Zweig, Eric. *It's a Numbers Game! Football.* National Geographic Kids Books, 2022.

INDEX

Boldface indicates illustrations.

A

Aboriginal people 123
Adaptive bikes **68**
Algonquin tribe 47
Archery 62-63, **62-63**, 114
Automobile racing 96, **96**, 97, **97**

B

Badminton 77, **77**
Balance beam 81, **81**, 121
Baseball 6, 24-27, **24-27**, 125
Basketball 6, **10**, 12-17, **12-17**, 55, **113**, 114, 125
Bicycle motocross (BMX) 68, **68**
Bobsledding 110, **111**, 116, **116**
Boomerangs 123, **123**
Bowling 64-65, **64-65**, 125
Bows and arrows 62-63, **62-63**
Bull's-eyes 63, **63**

C

Caber toss 122
Capoeira 122, **122**
Cheerleading 48-49, **48-49**
Climbing walls **78**, 79, **79**
Cricket 52-53, **52-53**, 125

Curling **98**, 100-101, **100-101**, 125
Cycling 68-69, **68-69**, **115**, 120, 125

D

Discus throw 95
Diving 87, **87**, 125
Donkey racing 123, **123**
Double Dutch 59, **59**
Duckpin bowling 65, **65**

E

Egypt, ancient 64, 67

F

Fencing 70-71, **70-71**
Field hockey **43**, 44-45, **44-45**
Figure skating 102-103, **102-103**, 116, **117**, 121, 125
Flag football 21, **21**
Flying discs 54, **54**, 55
Football 6, **10**, 18-23, **18-23**, 55, 125
Formula 1 racing 97, **97**
Four Square 59, **59**
Freestyle skiing 106, **106**

G

Goalball 119, **119**
Golf **60**, 72-73, **72-73**, 125

Greece, ancient 44, 67, 92, 113
Gymnastics 48, 55, 80-81, **80-81**, 114, 120

H

Half-pipes 108, **108**
High jump 94, 95
Highland Games 122
Hurdles **60**, 93

I

Ice hockey 6, 36-41, **36-41**, 116, **116**, 125
Ice skating **99**, 103, **104**, 105; see also Figure skating; Speed skating
IndyCar racing 96, **96**

J

Jai alai 122, **122**
Javelin throw **94**, 95
Judo 83, **83**
Jumping rope 59, **59**

K

Kabaddi 58, **58**
Karate 82-83, **82-83**
Kickball 58, **58**

L

Lacrosse 46-47, **46-47**
Long jump 94, **94**
Luge 111, **111**

M

Marathons 92, 123
Martial arts 82-83, **82-83**, 122, **122**
Motocross 97, **97**; see also Bicycle motocross
Motorcycle racing 96, **96**, 97, **97**
Motorsports 96-97, **96-97**

N

Naismith, James 13
NASCAR 96
Native Americans 47

O

Olympic Games 67, 92, **112-117**, 113-117

P

Paralympics 118-119, **118-119**
Pickleball 77, **77**
Ping-Pong 76, **76**
Playground sports 58-59, **58-59**
Pole vault 94, **94-95**
Pond hockey 37, **37**
Poppen, Sherman 108

R

Racket sports 76-77, **76-77**; see also Tennis
Rings (gymnastics) 80, **80**
Rock climbing 78-79, **78-79**

Rodeo 122, **122**
Rowing 89, **89**
Rugby 50-51, **50-51**, 123
Running 92, **92, 93**, 112, **120-121**

S

Sailing 89, **89**, 120
Sepak Takraw 123, **123**
Shot put 95, **95**
Skateboarding 60, 90-91, **90-91**
Skeleton (sport) **110**, 111
Skiing 2-4, 106-107, **106-107**, 116, **116, 118**, 120
Sledding **98**, 110-111, **110-111**
Snowboarding **99**, 108-109, **108-109**
Soccer **1, 5**, 6, 30-35, **30-35**, 114, 125
Softball 6, 28-29, **28-29**, 123
Special Olympics 120-121, **120-121**
Speed skating 104-105, **104-105, 112**
Sport climbing 78
Sports: definition 9
Springboards 87, 125
Squash 77, **77**
Stand-up paddleboarding 88, **88**
Stock car racing 96, **96**
Street hockey 39, **39**
Summer Olympics 114-115, **114-115**, 117

Surfing **61**, 84-85, **84-85**
Swimming 86-87, **86-87**, 112, 114, **114**, 120, **120**

T

Table tennis 76, **76**
Tennis **5**, 74-75, **74-75**, 125
Tour de France 69, **69**
Track and field **60**, 92-95, **92-95**, 112, 114, **120-121**

U

Ultimate (sport) 54-55, **54-55**

V

Vault (gymnastics) 81, **81**
Velodromes 68, 125
Volleyball **42**, 56-57, **56-57**, 114, 125

W

Walking 92
Water sports 88-89, **88-89**; see also Diving; Surfing; Swimming
Wheelchair sports **5, 113**, 118, **118, 119**
Winter Olympics 116-117, **116-117**
World map 122-123
Wrestling 66-67, **66-67**, 125

PHOTO CREDITS

COVER: (softball), sirtravelalot/SS; (football player), Beto Chagas/SS; (soccer celebration), AzmanL/GI; (track), SolStock/GI; (gymnast), Taxi/GI; (hockey skates), Alexander Mirokhin/AS; (bowling ball), 3desc/AS; (basketball hoop), Sports Images/DR; spine (lacrosse), C Squared Studios/GI; back cover (mountain biking), Thomas Barwick/GI; (birdie), Nikolai Sorokin/AS; **CHAPTER 1:** 1, Hemis/ASP; 2-3, Imgorthand/GI; 4 (UP), Tatiana Alexandrovna Mordvinova/DR; 4 (LE), Wayne Mckown/DR; 4 (RT), Ba dins/SS; 4-5 (Ch 1 background), Romaro Images/SS; 4-5 (Ch 1 background), Vadim Sazhniev/SS; 5 (UP), Steve Collender/SS; 5 (LO LE), Heinrich van den Berg/GI; 5 (LO RT), Kieran McManus/ASP; 8-9, Shoji Fujita/GI; 10 (UP LE), Mark Herreid/AS; 10 (UP RT), matimix/AS; 10 (LO LE), Stuart Monk/AS; 10 (RT), Glenda Powers/AS; 11 (UP LE), Gino Santa Maria/SS; 11 (UP RT), FatCamera/GI; 11 (LO LE), BillionPhotos/AS; 11 (LO RT), Stefan Balaz/SS; 12-13, Sergey Novikov/AS; 13, Jim West/ASP; 14, WavebreakMediaMicro/AS; 15, ferrantraite/GI; 16 (UP), Photodisc/National Geographic Image Collection; 16 (LO), Brocreative/SS; 16-17, Anucha Tiemsom/SS; 17, AB Forces News Collection/ASP; 18, Rich Graessle/Icon Sportswire via GI; 19 (UP), John Torcasio/ASP; 19 (LO), Nic Antaya/GI; 20, Michael Siluk/ASP; 21 (UP), Pete Saloutos/GI; 21 (LO), Derrick Neill/DR; 22 (UP), Mark Herreid/AS; 22 (LO), James Boardman/DR; 22-23, Alesandro14/SS; 23, Thomas Barwick/GI; 24, Zsolt Uveges/SS; 25 (UP), Pixel Pig/GI; 25 (LO), The Image Bank/GI; 26 (UP), Randy Hines/ASP; 26 (LO), Erik Isakson/GI; 26-27, Sanderson Design/SS; 27 (UP), Elliott Cowand Jr/SS; 28, Jon Osumi/SS; 29, Cal Sport Media/ASP; 30-31, Robin/ASP; 31, Ljupco Smokovski/AS; 32 (UP), stevedangers/ISP; 32 (CTR), Dusan Kostic/AS; 32 (LO), Monkey Business/AS; 33 (UP), Heinrich van den Berg/GI; 33 (CTR), Hero Images/GI; 34-35, iegor/AS; 35 (UP), Fabrizio Marian/DR; 35 (LO), Sergey Novikov/AS; 36-37, Julia Baturina/SS; 37, Jeff Whyte/DR; 38, Luca Santilli/SS; 39 (UP), Joshua Sarner/Icon Sportswire/GI; 39 (LO), FatCamera/GI; 40, Cmann Photo/ISP; 40-41, RNKO/AS; 41, Bruce Bennett/AP Images; **CHAPTER 2:** 42 (UP LE), Action Images/Jason O'Brien/Reuters/ASP; 42 (LO LE), Sergey Novikov/AS; 42 (LO RT), RTimages/AS; 42-43 (CTR), sirtravelalot/SS; 42-43 (Ch 2 background), ksuksu/AS; 43 (UP), Gerard Koudenburg/DR; 43 (LO), Photodisc /National Geographic Image Collection; 44-45, Chris Van Lennep/DR; 44, Claudia Harms-Warlies/SS; 45, Jeff Dalton/AS; 46-47, FatCamera/ISP; 47, Susan Leggett/ASP; 48, Mitchell Layton/GI; 48-49 (CTR), Moodboard/AS; 49 (RT), kali9/GI; 50, Sport Picture Library/ASP; 51, Paolo Bona/SS; 52 (UP), imagedb/AS; 52 (LO), Jjpixs/AS; 53 (UP), Kenneth William Caleno/SS; 53 (LO), Harry Trump-ICC/GI; 54-55, Black and Bright ph/AS; 55 (UP), Fairbanks Daily News-Miner/ZUMA Press/ASP; 55 (LO), Bob Daemmrich/ASP; 56-57, FatCamera/GI; 57 (UP), Michael Turner/SS; 57 (LO), Kathryn Scott Osler/GI; 58 (UP), Yellow Dog Productions/GI; 58 (LO), Snehal Jeevan Pailkar/SS; 59 (UP), Sipa US /ASP; 59 (LO), Dolores Harvey/AS; **CHAPTER 3:** 60 (UP LE), Jim Arbogast/GI; 60 (UP RT), Hutangach/AS; 60 (LO LE), Erik Isakson/GI; 60 (LO RT), Rmarmion/DR; 60-61 (Ch 3 background), NeMaria/SS; 61 (LO), Tropical studio/AS; 61 (LO), Denis Pepin/AS; 62-63, famveldman/AS; 63, Lucidio Studio, Inc./ASP; 64-65, Pixel-Shot/SS; 65 (UP), Dabarti CGI/SS; 65 (CTR), Konstantin Faraktinov/SS; 65 (LO), Tui Photoengineer/AS; 66-67, Vitalij Sova/DR; 67, AP Images/Brent Clark/CSM via ZUMA Wire; 68 (UP), Sollina Images/Blend Images/AS; 68 (LO), Pacific Press/GI; 69, Lya Cattel/GI; 70-71, Julian Pictures/AS; 71 (CTR), AlexLMX/ISP; 71 (LE), InterFoto/ASP; 71 (RT), Olekcii Mach/AS; 72 (UP), Robert Cicchetti/GI; 72 (CTR), Dasha Petrenko/SS; 73 (CTR), AlexPhototest/AS; 73 (LE), Ronnie Kaufman/The Image Bank RF/GI; 73 (RT), ifong/SS; 74, Take A Pix Media/Stocksy; 75 (UP), Ptaxa/GI; 75 (LO), Galina Barskaya/AS; 76, Jose Luis Pelaez/Corbis/VCG/GI; 77 (UP), Ahturner/SS; 77 (CTR), Light Poet/SS; 77 (LO), Crezalyn Nerona Uratsuji/GI; 78, Sergey Ryzhov/SS; 79 (UP), Tobias Arhelger/DR; 79 (LO), galitskaya/ISP; 80 (UP), CasarsaGuru/GI; 80 (CTR), master1305/AS; 81 (UP), Luigi Fardella/SS; 81 (LO), Image Source/GI; 82 (CTR), Satyrenko/SS; 82 (LO), New Africa/AS; 83 (UP), VVN/ASP; 83 (LO), Iakov Filimonov/ASP; 84 (UP), Mikalai Bachkou/AS; 84 (LO), KK Stock/SS; 84-85, Allison Joyce/GI; 86, cmcderm1/ISP; 87 (UP), PCN Photography/ASP; 87 (LO), Lawrence del Mundo/Stocksy/AS; 88, EvgeniiAnd/AS; 89 (UP), Rena Schild/SS; 89 (LO), Famveldman/DR; 90, MichaelSvoboda/GI; 91 (CTR), Nikokvfrmoto/AS; 91 (LO), Mike Blake/Reuters; 92 (UP), SolStock/GI; 92 (LO), Olga Evans/SS; 92-93, SolStock/ISP; 94 (UP), SolStock/GI; 94 (LO), EvrenKalinbacak/SS; 94-95, Mark Nolan/GI; 95, WavebreakMediaMicro/AS; 96 (UP), Whpics/DR; 96 (LO LE), Christian Petersen/GI; 96 (LO RT), HodagMedia/SS; 97 (UP), TonyB/ASP; 97 (LO), Cristiano Barni/SS; **CHAPTER 4:** 98 (UP), Ariel Skelley/GI; 98 (LO LE), Xinhua/Sipa USA/ASP; 98 (LO RT), Mega Pixel/SS; 98-99 (Ch 4 background), incomible/AS; 99 (UP LE), Microgen/AS; 99 (UP CTR), J. Helgason/SS; 99 (LO), Peter Gudella/SS; 99 (RT), Ivan Ekushenko/DR; 100, Elena Nichizhenova/SS; 101, Robert Przybysz/AS; 102-103, Svetlana Lazarenka/ASP; 103, vnlit/SS; 104-105, Ivan Danru/AS; 105 (UP), Chelsdo/DR; 105 (CTR), Photopat/ASP; 105 (LO), Yusuke Nakanishi AFLO SPORT/ASP; 106 (UP), Artur Didyk/SS; 106 (LO), Arief Juwono/GI; 107 (UP), Gorilla Images/SS; 107 (LO), mmphoto/GI; 107 (RT), Billion Photos/SS; 108, Mjaud/SS; 108-109, Ahturner/SS; 110 (UP), Alexandra Beier/Reuters/GI; 110 (CTR), Ron Nickel/GI; 111 (UP), Jeff Smith - Perspectives/SS; 111 (LO), Chuck Myers/MCT/Alamy Live News/ASP; **CHAPTER 5:** 112 (UP LE), Pavel Byrkin/DR; 112 (UP RT), Marcello Farina/Southcreek/ZUMA Press/ASP; 112 (LO LE), Martin Meissner/AP Images; 112 (LO RT), Anja Niedringhaus/AP Images; 112-113 (Ch 5 background), OlgaKlyushina/SS; 113 (UP), Yasuyoshi CHIBA/AFP via GI; 113 (LO), Morry Gash/AP Photo; 114 (UP), Pavel Byrkin/DR; 114 (LO), Takamitsu Mifune/Photo Kishimoto/DPPI/ASP; 115 (UP LE), Andre Ricardo/DR; 115 (UP RT), Wally Skalij/GI; 115 (LO), VCG/Stringer/GI; 116 (UP), FamVeld/SS; 116 (LO LE), Hkratky/DR; 116 (LO RT), Ron Hogan/DR; 117 (UP), Chine Nouvelle/SIPA/SS; 117 (LO), RvS.Media/Robert Hradil/GI; 118 (UP), PA Images/ASP; 118 (LO LE), Marco Ciccolella/SS; 118 (LO RT), Yasuyoshi Chiba/GI; 119 (UP), George Blonsky/ASP; 119 (LO), Lintao Zhang/GI; 120-121, Damian Dovarganes/AP Images; 120, Juan Carlos Ulate/Reuters; 121 (UP), Seonggwang Kim/AP Images; 121 (LO), Yves Herman/Reuters; 122 (UP), Polina Kobycheva/ASP; 122 (CTR), Alvis Upitis/ASP; 122 (LO), Vladimir/AS; 123 (UP), BTW Images/SS; 123 (CTR LE), Eric Lafforgue/ASP; 123 (CTR RT), Levranii/AS; 123 (LO), Luis Leamus/ASP; **END MATTER:** 125, Bigred/ASP; 128, Yanlev/AS

For all the kids who will put this book down and get out and play! —J. B.

The publisher acknowledges and thanks Rebecca Hudson at ESPN for her expert review of this book. Many thanks also to project manager Grace Hill Smith, researcher Michelle Harris, and photo editors Sharon Dortenzio and Lori Epstein for their invaluable help with this book.

Since 1888, the National Geographic Society has funded more than 14,000 research, conservation, education, and storytelling projects around the world. National Geographic Partners distributes a portion of the funds it receives from your purchase to National Geographic Society to support programs including the conservation of animals and their habitats. To learn more, visit natgeo.com/info.

For more information, visit nationalgeographic.com, call 1-877-873-6846, or write to the following address:

National Geographic Partners, LLC
1145 17th Street N.W.
Washington, DC 20036-4688 U.S.A.

For librarians and teachers: nationalgeographic.com/books/librarians-and-educators

More for kids from National Geographic: natgeokids.com

National Geographic Kids magazine inspires children to explore their world with fun yet educational articles on animals, science, nature, and more. Using fresh storytelling and amazing photography, *Nat Geo Kids* shows kids ages 6 to 14 the fascinating truth about the world—and why they should care. **natgeo.com/subscribe**

For rights or permissions inquiries, please contact National Geographic Books Subsidiary Rights: bookrights@natgeo.com

Designed by Nicole Lazarus, Design Superette

Library of Congress Cataloging-in-Publication Data

Names: Buckley, James, Jr., 1963- author.
Title: Little kids first big book of sports / James Buckley, Jr.
Description: Washington, D.C. : National Geographic Kids, 2023. | Series: Little kids first big book | Includes bibliographical references and index. | Audience: Ages 4-8 | Audience: Grades 2-3
Identifiers: LCCN 2022003612 | ISBN 9781426373220 (hardcover) | ISBN 9781426375118 (library binding)
Subjects: LCSH: Sports--Juvenile literature.
Classification: LCC GV705.4 .B84 2023 | DDC 796--dc23/eng/20220516
LC record available at https://lccn.loc.gov/2022003612

Printed in China
22/PPS/1